ICE HOCKEY LEGENDS

Wayne Gretzky

Brett Hull

Jaromir Jagr

Mario Lemieux

Eric Lindros

Mark Messier

CHELSEA HOUSE PUBLISHERS

ICE HOCKEY LEGENDS

BRETT HULL

Lou Friedman

CHELSEA HOUSE PUBLISHERS
Philadelphia

Produced by Daniel Bial and Associates
New York, New York

Picture research by Alan Gottlieb
Cover illustration by Bill Vann

First Printing

1 3 5 7 9 8 6 4 2

Library of Congress Cataloging-in-Publication Data

Friedman, Lou.
    Brett Hull / by Lou Friedman.
      p. cm. — (Ice hockey legends)
    Includes bibliographical references (p.) and index.
    Summary: The life story of the goal scorer for the St. Louis Blues who
followed in his father's footsteps and rose to ice hockey superstardom.
    ISBN 0-7910-4555-2
    1. Hull, Brett, 1964- —Juvenile literature. 2. Hockey players—Canada—
Biography—Juvenile literature. 3. St. Louis Blues (Hockey team)—Juvenile
literature. [1. Hull, Brett, 1964- . 2. Hockey players.] I. Title. II. Series.
GV848.5.H8F75   1997
796.962'092—dc21   97-27363
[B]   CIP
                                                                     AC

CONTENTS

THE 50-50 CLUB

People in hockey will tell you that most players are labeled by the style they play, regardless of size and skill. Some players are tagged as defensive-style players, some are more physical, and others are playmakers.

St. Louis Blues star Brett Hull knows his role, and it rarely changes. Hull's job is to score goals. Lots of them.

Hull does his job well. He scored 485 goals in his first 10 seasons in the National Hockey League (NHL) with the Calgary Flames and the St. Louis Blues. Of all those goals, Hull says that one of the most special came on January 25, 1991, in the Joe Louis Arena in Detroit.

It was the 49th game of the 1990-91 season, and Hull had 48 goals heading into the game against the Detroit Red Wings. Hull, who had suffered a sprained knee ten days earlier which forced him to miss the All-Star Game, was try-

After the 1990 game against the Toronto Maple Leafs, Brett Hull holds the puck he used to score his 50th goal of the season.

ing to become only the fifth player in NHL history to score 50 goals in 50 games. He would match the feat of Wayne Gretzky (who did it three times), Mario Lemieux, Mike Bossy, and Maurice "The Rocket" Richard.

To get into that elite group of talent, Hull needed two goals in two games. He had averaged exactly one goal per game so far in the season, but he could not suffer even a mild drop-off in performance without missing his objective.

Hull is not the kind of player to go seeking personal records, but he admitted that this one caused to him start thinking a little too much. "I was pressing," he said. "I wasn't having fun out there." Most of the time, someone watching Hull play can tell just by the expressions on his face that he's having more fun than almost any other player on the ice.

When the Red Wings shut Hull down early in that game, however, he was feeling butterflies in his stomach. "After the first period," Hull said, "I was kind of starting to get a little nervous."

Hull got his 49th goal late in the second period against Red Wings goalie Tim Cheveldae.

"Jeff Brown spotted me alone in the left circle," Hull said. "Defenseman Rick Zombo came out to meet me, and I ripped a shot past him and Cheveldae."

Hull did not need to wait for game number 50. He put his name in the record books early in the third period, on a pass from one of his favorite centers, Adam Oates.

"He picked up the puck 10 feet from the blue line and fed me a pass over the stick of a Red Wings player," Hull said. "Shot. Goal."

After scoring goal number 50, Hull was elated. "I couldn't even play in the rest of the third period," Hull said. "I was in dreamland."

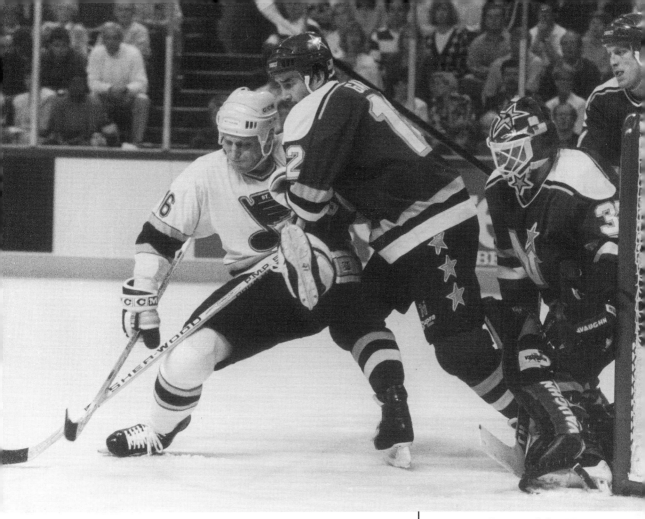

The fans in the Joe Louis Arena—the enemy's building—gave Hull a standing ovation. The Blues won the game 9-4.

That goal was one of the biggest parts of Brett Hull's best season in the National Hockey League. He wound up with a career-high 86 goals and added 45 assists for another career high of 131 points. The team reached the second round of the playoffs, and Hull wound up winning the Hart Trophy, an award voted on by hockey writers and given out by the National Hockey League for the most valuable player in the entire league during the regular season. He beat out such stars as Wayne Gretzky, Mario Lemieux, and Mark Messier, and in a 14-year span between

Stewart Gavin of the Minnesota North Stars tackles Brett Hull to prevent Hull from scoring. Gavin received a two-minute holding penalty.

1980 and 1993, those four players were the only ones to win that particular award.

Hull was very proud of his achievement, which put him in a select class of hockey player. "To be alongside Richard, Bossy, Gretzky, and Lemieux is quite an honor," he said. "Especially when you consider who hasn't done it."

His father turned the trick, but he did so in the World Hockey Association, a league that lasted from 1972 through 1979 before four teams (Edmonton, Quebec, Winnipeg, and Hartford) joined the NHL and the rest simply went out of existence. Bobby Hull never managed the 50-50 feat in the National Hockey League.

"There are great NHL scorers who have never reached that mark," said Brett. "Also amazing is that I'm only the third player to do it in less than 50 games."

Gretzky scored 50 goals in just 39 games during the 1981-82 season, and he did it twice more (in 42 games and 49 games). Lemieux, in the 1988-89 season, tallied 50 goals in 46 games.

According to Hull, he's not getting those 50 markers without some help. "I think about how many guys have to work together to create the chances for my goals," he said. "I'm not a flashy player who creates his own chances; I need someone to get me the puck.

"The night I got my 50th goal," he continued, "Bob Bassen, Rich Sutter, and Scott Stevens worked like crazy to get the puck out of our zone. No one talked about it, yet clearly everyone worked to help me reach the milestone."

To prove it wasn't a fluke, the very next season, Hull did it again, although it took him the full 50 games to reach 50 goals. It was a year and three days later, on January 28, 1992, during a 3-3 tie, in Los Angeles when Hull hit the half-century mark against Kings goalie Kelly Hrudey.

In 1996, Hull scored his 500th National Hockey League goal, joining 24 other players in achieving that milestone. One of those two dozen players who hit that mark was his father, Bobby, who wound up with 610 goals.

MY DAD'S A HOCKEY PLAYER

In his heyday, Bobby Hull was just as much of a standout in the hockey world as Brett Hull is today. Bobby blazed a lot of trails in hockey. He was the first player to put a curve in his stick blade, making an already dangerous slapshot even scarier for opposing goalies. He never turned away a fan's request for an autograph, displaying amazing patience with those whose dollars supported both himself and the sport he played.

Bobby Hull, born on January 3, 1939, was one of 11 children. He grew up on a farm in Pointe Anne, Ontario. He helped out on the farm while growing up, taking on such tasks as raising cattle and performing the usual farm chores such as pitching hay and mending fences.

When Bobby was growing up, many families in his area had a weekly ritual throughout the hockey season. Every Saturday night, they gathered around the radio (and later, the television)

A jubilant Bobby Hull shouts at a fan as his Chicago Blackhawks are moments away from winning the 1961 Stanley Cup. Eric Nesterenko is at right.

Even in the later years of his career, Bobby Hull was a commanding figure on the ice. Here he skates past a young Brad Park of the New York Rangers.

to listen to Foster Hewitt broadcast the Toronto Maple Leafs games. Saturday night was "Hockey Night in Canada," and the broadcasts were given the same name.

"Those games meant so much to us," the elder Hull recalled. "We'd be out on the ice the next day, pretending we were Maurice Richard, Elmer Lach, and Gordie Howe playing in Maple Leaf Gardens."

Bobby also cherished those rare times when his parents would make the trip to Toronto with Bobby in tow to see the Maple Leafs in person.

"I'll never forget," Hull said. "We'd have to stand in line for what seemed like an eternity, but then we'd finally get tickets. I'd run ahead, up the stairs to the balcony, where I'd always try to get a place on the railing [for standing room only] and hold my arms out to save a place for Mum and Dad."

Hull, who would eventually play both against and alongside Howe, even got his autograph. "I waited after the game to get Gordie Howe's autograph," Hull said. "When Gordie came out, I was afraid to walk up to him. But my dad pushed me and said, 'Go ahead, go ahead, it's all right.' I did, and I'll never forget how much that autograph meant to me."

Hull signed with the Chicago Blackhawks in 1957 and set a Chicago milestone as the youngest player the team ever signed. He played center for two years and then was switched to left wing, where he made his name scoring goals in bushels.

In the 1961-62 season, Hull became only the third player in NHL history to score 50 goals in a season, tying him with Richard and Bernie "Boom-Boom" Geoffrion. He scored most of those goals while racing down the left side of the ice, blond hair flying in the wind, and unleashing one of his cannonball blasts, which sometimes reached speeds of up to 120 miles per hour. Hull broke the 50-goal mark in the 1965-66 season, when he beat New York Ranger goalie Cesare Maniago. In the hockey world, Hull's hitting goal number 51 was comparable to when Roger Maris broke Babe Ruth's single-season home-run record by hitting his 61st. Hull wound up with 54 goals that season, and later scored 52 goals (1966-67) and a career-high 58 (1968-69). Hull hit the 50-goal mark five times in his career and was named an All-Star in 12 of his 14 NHL seasons, including the last nine he played.

Hull was a proud man, and he felt that the Blackhawks lied to him about a new contract. With the newly formed World Hockey Association (WHA) ready to roll in the fall of 1972, Hull took a look at what they had to offer. If the new league was to establish itself against the historical National Hockey League, its best bet would be to sign a few of the top NHL players. The only way to do that was to offer them more money than they had ever seen in their lifetime. That's why several NHL stars at the time—including Howe, Gerry Cheevers, Derek Sanderson, and Bernie Parent— made the jump to the new league. That league also was the starting place for current NHL stars such as Wayne Gretzky, Mark Messier, and Mike Gartner.

Hull cashed in on this new venture by signing with the Winnipeg Jets for nearly $3 million. Not only did he like the money, but he also was glad to make his home base back in Canada. For years, he and his family had spent most of their time in Chicago, although they spent summers in Ontario. Now the Hulls had a new home in Winnipeg.

The senior Hull made a name for himself alongside two Swedes that the Jets signed for their offensive skills. The line of Ulf Nilsson at center, Hull at left wing, and Anders Hedberg at right wing was the best in the WHA. They all could skate like the wind. Hull still had his dangerous slapshot as a weapon, Nilsson was a great passer, and Hedberg could score from practically anywhere on the ice. Together, they were probably the best line ever to play in the WHA.

The young league was facing problems. Trying to compete with the NHL, the WHA set up teams in major metropolises: New York, Chicago, and Los Angeles. None of them survived for long. The WHA also tried to place teams in markets that had never had hockey before (such as Miami, Florida, and Birmingham, Alabama) and cities that cared little about minor league teams already in place (such as Cincinnati and San Francisco). A bigger problem for the WHA was the increase in violence in the league.

Hull's two linemates were constantly abused both physically and verbally by opposing players because of the prejudice that existed then toward European players, especially Swedes. Hull sat out a game in protest, hoping his stand would cause the league to create tougher penalties for such abuse. Hull got a lot of publicity, and even some sympathy, but in the end, the league did very little to stem the tide of the growing physical play taking over in hockey.

Hull finished his career with the Hartford Whalers. He played nine games for them in the 1979-80 season and scored five goals. He retired after failing to reach a contract agreement with the Whalers. All in all, he played in 1,063 NHL regular season games and scored 610 goals. He added 62 playoff goals in 119 games, for a total of 672 NHL goals. He also won one Stanley Cup championship with Chicago in 1961.

He also had some children, one of whom would follow in his footsteps.

GROWING UP

After Bobby retired, both Chicago and Winnipeg retired his jersey, meaning that no one else who plays for those teams will ever wear number nine. But Hull accomplished more than his 610 NHL goals and entrance into the Hall of Fame.

He and his wife Joanne raised a big family—five children, to be exact: Bobby Jr., Blake, Brett, Bart, and Michelle. With the kids having a hockey-playing father and a figure-skating mother, one might think that all four boys would soon be following in their father's footsteps and wind up playing in the NHL. Only one of the four ever got that far, and it was the least likely: Brett.

Brett was born on August 9, 1964, in Belleville, Ontario, site of the Hull family summer retreat. He was the only one of the five kids born in Canada. He wasn't fond of hockey in his youth: he

The Hull family didn't always put three straws in one glass of milk. When Bobby broke his jaw and had to have it wired shut while it healed, they all shared liquid meals with him. That's Brett on the right.

would get cold at the rink and want to get off the ice, or he would skip the pregame warm-up rituals of skating and shooting because he felt they were a waste of time.

Hull was not exactly a great skater at an early age. When he was four years old, once a referee had to carry him to the face-off circle because he couldn't get there on his own in a timely fashion. Finally, the referee let him stay in the offensive zone near the net. Still, there were early signs of skill. Brett scored the winning goal in that game.

Joanne once chided her son for not giving her enough credit. "I kept reading that you inherited all your ability from your father," she said to Brett. "Have you forgotten that I was a professional skater? I'm the one who taught you how to skate."

Brett responded, "Mom, I'm actually doing you a favor by not crediting you for my skating. It's the worst part of my game!"

While playing on an outdoor rink in Elmhurst, Illinois, Brett found an interesting way to practice shooting accurately. He lined up some pucks on the ice and fired them at passing subway trains.

When Brett was seven, his father signed with the Jets, and the family moved to Winnipeg. That gave Brett, along with older brothers Bobby Jr. and Blake, a lot of free time to spend at the rink. The best place to learn how to play hockey is at a rink, and Brett got an education that no one could put a price on.

Throughout his junior hockey career, Bobby Jr. took a lot of physical and verbal heat for being the son of a legend. Not only did he get it from opponents, but coaches, reporters, and even

Bobby Hull officiates at a bike race, pitting (left to right) Bobby Jr., Blake, and Brett against one another.

teammates insisted on comparing him to his father while Bobby Jr. was trying to establish his own identity.

Blake and Brett also had to put up with tough comparisons, but Bobby Jr. was able to help them not be overwhelmed by it. In junior hockey, Blake and Brett suffered less from snipes and opponents who wanted to shut a Hull down on the ice.

Brett's younger brother Bart chose a different road than hockey: he made football his sport. Brett says that Bart "is the best athlete in the family." Bart attended Boise State University in Idaho, where he saw limited action at running back until his junior year, when he scored seven touchdowns as a short-yardage back. He was drafted in the first round by the British Columbia Lions of the Canadian Football League.

Michelle, the only female sibling in the family, is also the youngest. She's an orthopedic surgeon.

When the boys got bitten by the hockey bug at early ages, it was their mother who taught them how to skate—their dad was busy playing and earning a living. It was Bobby Sr. who taught Brett and his other sons how to play—not by taking them on the ice and instructing them, but by telling them to watch what he did.

Brett picked up a lot of moves from his father, but he had an easier time replicating Bobby's shot than his skating ability. "He was so graceful," Brett said, "yet he didn't look like he was putting any effort into his skating. He was like a panther: power and grace harmonized in one perfectly proportioned body. He was beautiful to watch and dangerous to defend against."

Although Hull got a hockey education most kids only dreamed about, his education took an abrupt turn at the age of 13, when Bobby and Joanne separated. Joanne took all five kids and moved out west to Vancouver, British Columbia.

Divorce is always tough on the family, mostly the children. When your father is a famous athlete, and you're trying to make it in that same sport, you become an easy target for insults from opposing players and fans. It only became worse because the papers reported daily on the goings on, which were getting more bitter as time passed.

"Folks get divorced," Brett said. "You can't do anything about it."

Joanne got remarried in 1982 to Harry Robinson, an accountant.

Brett saw little of his father in those days. "He wasn't around, but it wasn't his fault," Hull said. "Our relationship wasn't Ward Cleaver and the Beaver. Our relationship didn't end; it was just put on hold by circumstances.

"Our story is the unfortunate, all too common tale about how a divorce breaks up a family," he continued. "It was distance and circumstance that kept Dad and me apart—nothing more and nothing less. Divorce, by its nature, undermines relationships. When one parent isn't even in the same time zone, it makes contact even more difficult. It's always the kids that get caught in the middle."

The effects of the divorce on Brett were not hard to see. His grades in school suffered, and he didn't take care of himself physically. At one point, his weight shot up past 220 pounds. He was drifting, with no set purpose in life, when Rick Kozuback entered the picture.

Kozuback was the coach of a British Columbia Junior Hockey League team, the Penticton Knights. He knew that Hull was not in shape and had a questionable attitude. He also knew that Hull had a shot that few people other than his father Bobby possessed. So he offered Hull a spot on the team if Hull got himself into shape. Hull found out later that Kozuback was more interested in luring one of Hull's boyhood friends to his team and used Hull's possible presence on the team as an enticement.

Hull wasn't initially interested in moving five hours away from Vancouver to play for a slim chance to further his hockey career. After a long talk with his mom, Hull relented and headed northeast, all 226 pounds of him.

Brett knew that the main reason he had the offer was because of his father. "They told me that they were keeping me around because my name is Hull," he said. "One of their marketing strategies was to tell the fans they had a chance to watch Bobby Hull's son play."

Brett knew that his father's name would only carry him so far. So he worked himself into shape, practiced harder, and made an impression on Kozuback. Hull scored 48 goals that first season (1982-83) with Penticton, earning him a rookie-of-the-year award. The next season, he had 50 goals by Christmas. The league record for the most goals in one season was 83, held by Cliff Ronning, who is now with the Phoenix Coyotes. Hull wound up scoring 105 goals in just 56 games.

"If anybody else ever complained about how much I shot the puck," Hull said, "I had a stock answer: 'It's difficult to score without shooting the puck.'"

Hull did also pass the puck, as he added 83 assists for a total of 188 points. That broke by five points a league record set by John Newberry, who played 22 total games over four seasons with the Montreal Canadiens and Hartford Whalers.

Those two seasons with Penticton gave Hull a sense that he could make a career out of playing hockey. After the season, he would find out just how far he might go.

Kozuback was a master at getting his kids scholarships to play college hockey, and his reputation was tested by Hull. Hull's attitude toward school changed while he was playing under Kozuback. Hull wanted to get an education in case his hockey career went nowhere.

After the season, Hull was drafted by the Calgary Flames in the sixth round of the NHL entry draft. He also, through Kozuback, was offered a scholarship to play for the University of Minnesota-Duluth Bulldogs.

He wound up doing both.

4

BULLDOGS & FLAMES

Hull was excited about going to college. Three schools were hoping to obtain Hull's services: Colorado College, the University of North Dakota, and the University of Minnesota-Duluth, all schools with major hockey programs. Michigan State was interested in Hull early in the season, but dropped out when they decided he wasn't a good enough skater.

As in college football and basketball, hockey players are not exempt from recruiting. Constant phone calls, post cards, letters, and brochures found their way to Hull's home. "Being recruited by colleges was more exciting than being drafted [by Calgary]," Hull said. "It was nice to be wanted for my talent more than my surname."

Minnesota-Duluth recruited the most, and that impressed Hull. The fact that the hockey team was ranked high in the country also was a selling point, as was coach Mike Sertich. Hull also loved the small-town feel of Duluth. He was

Brett shows off the uniform he wore as a member of the Minnesota-Duluth Bulldogs.

hooked, but he had to make sure of one point with his future coach before signing with the Bulldogs.

"When I come to Duluth, I'm coming as Brett Hull, not Bobby Hull's son," Hull told Sertich.

Sertich replied, "We recruited Brett Hull. We think he's a much better player than Bobby Hull's son." Sold.

Playing in Duluth also appealed to Hull, so much so that he now has an off-season home there. "It has a big city's hustle, without losing the charm and ease of small-town life," Hull said. "Yes, you freeze all that's dear to you in the winter. But the payback is the most pleasant summer climate known to man. The nation could be drenched in sweat from a coast-to-coast heat wave, and Duluth would be 75 degrees with a cool breeze blowing off Lake Superior."

Hull found Sertich to be a demanding but fair coach. He stressed the importance of skating, never a Hull strong suit. Every Monday and Wednesday the team practiced without pucks.

"For 45 to 50 minutes, he skated us like a drill sergeant taking his recruits through basic training," Hull recalled. "I hated it, but I needed it."

What Hull also hated but needed was the dry land or off-ice training Sertich demanded. Hull, who reported to UM-D in less than top shape, found himself going out for what Sertich called "a little run." Sertich's definition of a little run was to do six miles in 45 minutes.

Hull was one of two players that year who didn't make it in time, but Hull said that he needed the push Sertich gave if he was ever going to improve as a player. "I went to UM-D because Sertich's practices were tough," Hull said. "When he recruited me, I told him I wanted to improve on my skating and defense. He promised me I would, and his word was good. He pushed me hard."

Hull also found his coach to be adaptable to his players' strongest assets. "He didn't try to change the way I played the game," Hull explained. "He said, 'If you are a thoroughbred, I won't try to make you into a plow horse.'"

Hull also praised Sertich as a great teacher of the game. "I learned more in my first season in Duluth than I learned in all the previous years I had played hockey," Hull said.

Hull also started missing his father a bit more. He tacked up in his locker an old hockey trading card of his father for inspiration, and longed for his dad to see him play. He got his wish when Bobby called to tell him he would watch his son play in the 1985 quarterfinal playoff series.

After an initial slow start in his first season in Minnesota, Hull breezed through the year, finishing with 32 goals and 28 assists for 60 points. More importantly, UM-D was doing so well that they earned the number one college ranking. In a span covering late January to early March, the Bulldogs won 11 straight games. Hull's best weekend was spent playing Wisconsin, where he had back-to-back hat tricks (games where he scored three goals or more).

Hull and the Bulldogs made college hockey's version of the "Final Four," where they faced Rensselaer Polytechnic Institute, who had, on their squad, one of Hull's future teammates, center Adam Oates. Hull scored one goal during regulation time, but after 60 minutes the Bulldogs and Engineers were tied 5-5.

Coach Mike Sertich said that he wanted Brett Hull, not "Bobby Hull's son," to come to Minnesota-Duluth.

Matt Christensen was the center of Brett Hull's line in college. When Christensen suffered a stroke, the team lost early in the playoffs.

The previous season, the Bulldogs had made the final game, where they lost to Bowling Green in a four-overtime game. This game looked to be a repeat of that marathon, as after two overtimes, the score was still tied at five. However, a scuffle at the end of the second overtime period gave RPI a power play (when an opponent is serving a penalty) in the third overtime. With Hull's Bulldogs down a man, the Engineers manufactured a goal and a win.

The following season, the Bulldogs were able to put their heartbreaking loss behind them, as they won 13 of their first 16 games. Hull was on fire virtually all season long. He wound up with 52 goals and 32 assists for 84 points, even though he played six fewer games than the previous season.

The Bulldogs were fighting for the top spot late in the season when hockey took a back seat to life. Hull's center, Matt Christensen, suffered a stroke. That devastated the entire team. With their minds never fully in the game, they lost their last four matches. Christensen eventually recovered and even visited the team before the playoffs began. Nevertheless, the Bulldogs lost in the second round.

"Sertich tried to keep our spirits up, but we were toast," Hull said. "We had lost the will to win, and he knew it."

After two years of college hockey, Hull knew that he had a better shot of making it to the NHL than ever before. He asked Brian Burke to advise him on his options.

Burke at the time was a player agent. Since Hull was still in college, NCAA rules meant that if he signed with an agent, he'd lose his scholarship. He was allowed to have Burke as an advisor. This way, if he couldn't agree to a professional contract with the Flames, he would retain his college scholarship eligibility.

Although Sertich wasn't in favor of Hull turning pro after just two seasons at UM-D, he gave his blessing if Hull could secure a big contract. The Calgary Flames still had the rights to Hull and were close to being a serious contender for the Stanley Cup. All they needed was an extra goal scorer to give them an extra edge.

Burke made one statement of advice to Hull: if Calgary didn't offer him a one-way contract, Hull should turn the offer down and go back to the Bulldogs for another season. A one-way contract means that the player earns the same salary whether he plays in the NHL or in the minor leagues. Most youngsters signing their first pro contract have to sign a two-way contract, which means they get one particular salary when they play in the NHL and a significantly smaller salary if they play in the minors.

Calgary offered Hull a two-way contract, which he turned down. Two weeks later, Calgary offered a one-way deal. Hull signed a contract on a three-year deal plus an option. Calgary guaranteed to pay $70,000, then $105,000, then $115,000, and if they picked up the option, Hull would make $125,000. Calgary also gave Hull a signing bonus of $150,000.

At the time Hull signed, boys out of the three major Canadian junior leagues were held in higher regard by NHL general managers, who felt those players had more talent. It took a special college player to impress them, and it took a potential star to impress them enough to give him a one-way contract.

The Flames' coach was Bob Johnson, one of the leaders of the U.S. Hockey program. Johnson was always thinking about ways to improve his teams, and he was loved by his players for keeping a positive approach, even when circumstances were less than positive. He was known as a teacher who understood the value of patience. Since he was born in the United States and previously had a long career as the coach at the University of Wisconsin, Johnson knew the potential that college hockey players had. Johnson believed that Hull, despite a somewhat limited background, could really help the team.

Hull was trying to get acclimated to his new teammates and his new surroundings. That would be tough enough to do in training camp, but since Hull flew to Calgary to sign his contract and meet the press on May 5, he joined the team in the final stages of their run for the NHL championship. The Flames had just beaten Hull's future team, the St. Louis Blues, in a tough seven-game semifinal series, and now it would be the Flames and Montreal Canadiens competing for the right to skate around the ice holding the Stanley Cup, the oldest and most recognizable trophy in professional sports.

Hull was again somewhat out of shape, as he had gained 10 pounds between when the UM-D season ended and his NHL season started. After practice with the Flames, assistant coaches Bob Murdoch and Pierre Page skated Hull an extra hour to work off some of the weight and improve his conditioning. Hull observed the first two games of the finals from the Calgary press box, as the Flames won the first game 5-3 and lost the second game 3-2 in overtime.

Coach Johnson said that his team was exhausted and that there was a chance Hull

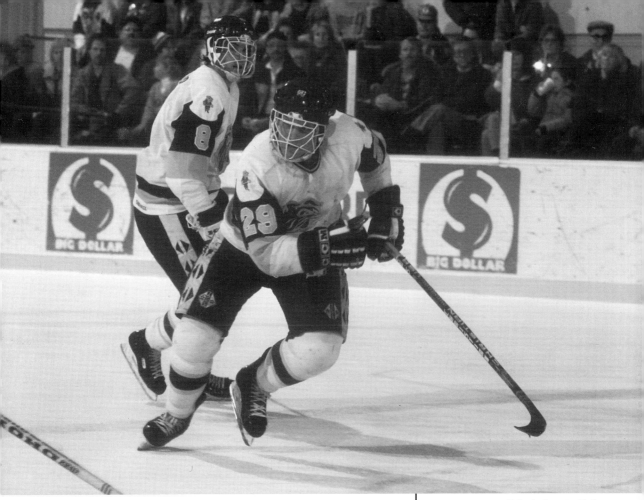

In 1985, Hull led the Bulldogs to a Final Four appearance in the NCAA hockey championships.

would play in Game 3 in Montreal. Hull was ecstatic when he heard the news. And true to his word, Johnson put Hull in the lineup. Officially, the date of Hull's National Hockey League debut was May 20, 1986. This was the first time that a rookie made his first-ever start in the Stanley Cup finals. (The only other player to find himself in that situation was Kelly Buchberger of the Edmonton Oilers, who did so a year after Hull.)

"I was in awe," Hull said of his Stanley Cup debut. "I was so nervous, I could barely lace my skates."

Hull's first shift came on Calgary's first power-play opportunity, and Hull fired a wrist shot that beat Montreal goaltender Patrick Roy (pronounced Rwa). Unfortunately, the puck rang off the post and did not go in the net. Hull officially ended the game with that one shot on goal, and the Flames lost the game 5-3. Hull was again inserted into the lineup for the fourth game, but he was blanked along with his teammates as Montreal won the game 1-0. Hull sat out the fifth and, as it turned out, final game of the series, as Montreal flew back to Calgary and won the Stanley Cup with a 4-3 victory.

When the next training camp opened in early September, Hull thought he would make the team. He made it through all of training camp and flew to Boston with the team for their opening game. But on the day of the game, at the team's morning skate (a ritual in which a team skates leisurely for about 45 minutes to get their legs ready for that night's game), Johnson told Hull that he was being sent to the Flames' minor league team in Moncton, New Brunswick. There were 17 forwards on the roster, and Johnson thought that Hull should spend a few weeks playing in the minors rather than sit in the NHL press boxes and just watch. He told Hull to work on his conditioning and defensive play; he also promised that the pro scouts would watch him in case other players suffered injuries or prolonged slumps and the team needed replacements.

When Hull arrived in New Brunswick, he discovered the coach there had an entirely different reputation than Johnson's. "I was out of there to Moncton to play for some guy who had a reputation that read like a Stephen King horror story," Hull said of his new coach, Terry Crisp.

Crisp was an old-school hockey player. He got by on hard work and guts, traits Hull didn't yet possess, by his own admission. Crisp survived

11 seasons in the NHL with the Boston Bruins, St. Louis Blues, New York Islanders, and Philadelphia Flyers. Crisp wore two Stanley Cup rings thanks to the time he spent with the Flyers.

Crisp admits that he made some mistakes when he was coaching in the Calgary system, and he has learned from those mistakes. Crisp's game was based on intensity and hard work—factors that had been crucial in his own success as an athlete. He was not interested in making friends with all his players, and Hull was particularly unhappy with his coach. "If you could do a million sit-ups, chin-ups, and pushups, the Flames coaches believed you were a good player," Hull recalled. "If you couldn't, the coaches thought you were bad. To that way of thinking, I was a bad player—very bad.

"It never seemed to matter how well I did on the ice," he continued. "They seemed to care more about physical prowess than offensive production. I was labeled a bad player unless I won an aerobics contest."

At first, Hull struggled under Crisp's demanding ways, as he scored only eight goals in his first 29 games. "He wanted to break my spirit," Hull said. "He wanted to change my life and my playing style, simply because he didn't like them. My personal philosophy has always been to expend more brain energy than body energy. I'm not real intense—I'm not intense at all."

Nevertheless, Hull started to catch fire and score more goals—but he was not enjoying himself. "I learned a tough lesson in Moncton—how to work for a boss who disliked my approach to both life and hockey," Hull said. "I had a 50-goal season and was miserable for most of it. What I learned in almost two seasons with Crisp was

After Hull signed with the Calgary Flames, he found himself playing for one of the toughest coaches in the business, Terry Crisp.

that I would never again play in a situation where the game stops being fun."

Despite his early struggles, Hull was called back up to Calgary. He played his first regular season game on November 14, 1986, when the Flames hosted the Hartford Whalers. Although his father didn't make the game, his mother and stepfather were there. What they saw excited them greatly. Brett scored the game-winning goal against Hartford netminder Steve Weeks.

Hull stuck around for three more games before Johnson sent him back to Moncton and Crisp. His performance at Moncton earned him the Dudley Garret Award as rookie of the year in the American Hockey League.

At the end of the season, Hull was again called up to Calgary, where he played in their playoff series against Winnipeg. He had two goals and an assist as the Flames were eliminated by the Jets. Hull then went back to Moncton to join in their playoff run, where in three games he scored twice and had two assists.

Johnson quit as Calgary's coach after the season to take a job as director of the U.S. Amateur Hockey program. Crisp was promoted to Johnson's spot, which meant that Hull's NHL career was in the hands of the coach whom he liked least.

Crisp kept Hull with the Flames throughout the 1987-88 season, but he didn't make life easy for him. Hull split time between the ice and the press box. He won the NHL rookie of the month award in November, when he had eight goals and six assists in 12 games. Ironically, Hull spent much of early December merely watching games from the press box. Crisp benched him for a perceived lack of effort. Hull never saw a regular period of ice time for the next three months, playing two games, then sitting out two, then playing one, then sitting out two more.

It all turned around on March 7, 1988. Hull was heading to the rink when Crisp summoned him into his office for a brief meeting. Crisp informed the rookie that he had been traded to St. Louis.

"When Terry Crisp told me I had been traded, I couldn't stop smiling," Hull said. "I had to put my head down, because the grin wouldn't go away."

Out of Crisp's presence, Hull let out a whoop. Blues fans would soon follow suit.

HAPPILY SINGING THE BLUES

Officially, league records have the deal as follows: Hull and fellow winger Steve Bozek were traded to the St. Louis Blues in exchange for defenseman Rob Ramage and goalie Rick Wamsley. Unofficially, the deal was also the first day of Hull's NHL career.

"In Calgary, it was a veteran team, and I didn't feel a part of things," Hull said. "I knew they were on the verge of winning a championship, but I didn't mind leaving."

There was one main reason why Hull was glad to leave. "It's really hard to play hockey knowing that when you make an error, you're going to get ripped. You're trying to learn. You don't feel good when the coach is just ripping you."

Despite riding the bench much of his rookie season, Hull still managed to score 26 goals for

Hull became a star soon after being traded to the St. Louis Blues. Here Mario Lemieux tries to pull him down before Hull has a chance at a breakaway goal.

Brett Hull is interviewed with his dad after they became the first father-son combination to each score 50 goals in a season.

the Flames in 52 games. Still, that wasn't good enough for Crisp.

Hull recounted that just before the trade, Flames general manager Cliff Fletcher, who swore that he would never trade a young prospect, held a meeting with his coaches and scouts and asked them the following question: "Are we prepared to do this trade, knowing that Brett Hull can score 160 goals in the next four seasons?" He then repeated the question, changing the number of goals to 180 and then 200.

Each time, the coaching staff and scouts unanimously answered yes.

Fletcher once even told the media that he thought Hull would score 180 goals in the next four seasons. If that was his thought, Hull wondered, why would they trade him? (Fletcher was slightly off in his prediction. Hull wound up scoring 199 goals in only three seasons!)

Hull finished the 1987-88 season by scoring six goals in 13 games for St. Louis, tallying a total of 32 goals in his rookie season. The Blues were in the playoffs that season, and Hull, in a sign of things to come, scored seven goals and added two assists in 10 postseason games.

Hull was happy with his new home. In November 1988, he found himself paired with new center Peter Zezel, who had been acquired from Philadelphia. Hull, who now had all the ice time he wanted under new coach Brian Sutter, clicked right away with Zezel. Hull's new center got him the puck in the best possible places to score, and score he did. Hull wound up with 41 goals and 43 assists for the season, 84 points in all. In the playoffs, Hull added five goals and five assists in 10 games.

Hull was flying high—that is, until a final meeting with Sutter before departing for the summer. "He made some general comments, and then he gave me his most serious look," Hull said. "He said to me, 'I don't want to insult you, but if you thought you were a good player last season, I hope you will think again. You can come back and score another 41 goals again, or you can take the next step up and score 65 and be a dominant NHL player. You can be a lot better than you are.'"

The difference between Sutter and Crisp was like night and day. "This wasn't Terry Crisp asking me to change my personality and completely revamp my game," Hull said. "This was a coach who let me play the way I wanted to play."

Hull respected Sutter for just that reason. "He's one of the most intense hockey people I've ever met," Hull said. "I'm probably one of the least intense hockey people he's ever met. Although Brian has a type-A personality and I have a type-Z personality, our relationship couldn't be better. He understands that my carefree attitude doesn't translate into a lack of desire on the ice. And it may not be his way, but he appreciates that I play best when I'm having fun."

That meeting elicited a promise from Hull to come to the next training camp in the best shape of his life, to give him a chance to get those 65 goals. He also was asked to provide more of a leadership role, simply because he was one of the most popular guys in the dressing room. Finally, Hull's contract was due to expire after the next season. The better he played, the fatter the new contract.

The only possible disappointment for Hull in the 1988-89 season was that his old team in Calgary wound up winning the Stanley Cup. Hull missed out on being on a championship team, but he didn't regret it.

"I wanted to play, plain and simple," Hull said of not being on the Flames when they won it all. "The championship would not have meant anything if I had been watching it from the press box."

Before Hull reported to training camp, the Blues sent him a contract offer. As Burke was no longer acting as an agent, Hull signed on with Bob Goodenow. (Goodenow is currently the representative for the National Hockey League Players' Association.) Goodenow and Blues management dickered back and forth for nine months. During that time, Hull strengthened his

bargaining position for money the best way he knew how: he scored 72 goals!

That number set an NHL record for the most goals by a right wing, surpassing Edmonton's Jari Kurri, who tallied 71 four years prior to Hull. He became only the sixth player in league history to hit the 70-goal mark, along with Kurri, Wayne Gretzky, Mario Lemieux, Phil Esposito, and Bernie Nicholls.

The Blues offered ridiculously low sums of money early in the season, but as Hull racked up more and more goals, the Blues kept raising their offer. But while they made small increments in their offer, Goodenow was raising his requests by substantial amounts. When the Blues offered a $300,000 deal, Goodenow countered by ask-

Hull looks to stuff in a rebound against Blackhawks' goalie Ed Belfour as he is hooked by Chris Chelios in the 1993 playoffs.

ing for a $700,000 deal. The Blues sat and waited for Hull to collapse. After all, nobody could keep up a scoring tear all season.

Bad move for the Blues.

On March 2, 1990, Hull became only the third player in St. Louis history to pass the 100-point mark. Goodenow raised his financial demands yet again. Finally, the Blues sent an offer to Hull that would pay him $1.2 million for the first season of a multi-year deal, going up to $2 million in the last year.

Goodenow and Hull liked the numbers being thrown around, but they didn't like that most of the money was tied up in bonuses. Hull's base guaranteed salary would have only been $350,000. Hull and Goodenow said no and came back with a two-year, $2-million offer, plus a half-million dollar signing bonus. St. Louis said no.

Time was running out for the Blues. If they did not sign Hull to a contract by July 31, he would officially be declared a free agent and could sign with any team he chose. Finally, they made an offer Hull and Goodenow accepted. He inked a contract that would guarantee him $7.1 million, not counting bonuses, and would keep him in a St. Louis uniform for four years.

As his father had blazed a new salary trail in the WHA, Brett did the same in the NHL. His average salary was the third-highest in the league, behind Gretzky and Lemieux. During the following season, opponents skated up to him during play stoppages and thanked him for getting such a large amount, because it set the standard to which every other player could compare himself. That meant that if another player scored 113 goals over two seasons, he could reasonably expect to get the same salary that Hull was getting.

Two weeks after signing the deal, the Blues traded Hull's center and good friend Zezel to Washington. The Blues also made another deal, this one with Detroit for center Adam Oates.

Hull was very familiar with his new teammate. Hull rarely notices the opposition when he's playing, but when he was at UM-D and they faced RPI in the semifinals in his first season, one player stood out in his mind: a center who set an NCAA record with five assists that game—Adam Oates.

Hull wasn't upset at getting Oates, but he was upset that the Blues traded Bernie Federko to get him. Federko was as historically linked to the Blues as Mickey Mantle was to the New York Yankees. In a very short time, however, Hull and Oates meshed together like Batman and Robin.

"There was one point during the season, it was around the All-Star break, that the two of us combined for 80 points in 15 games," Hull said. "And we won 12 of those games."

Those 80 points broke down to 22 goals and 14 assists for Hull and 8 goals and 36 assists for Oates. What made Zezel and then Oates, and later on Craig Janney, so valuable to Hull was that their best asset was passing the puck to one of their wingers who was open. Hull had a great knack for drifting into an open spot, where one of his centers would feed him a perfect pass. Hull didn't always score on those plays, but more often than not, he did.

Hull worried at first about the implications of Oates being a right-handed shot. As a righty, it is easier for Oates to pass to his left side when skating toward the opponent's goal, since he would make a forehand motion to get the pass to his left winger. Like most players, Oates can

After scoring a goal, Brett Hull (second from left) is congratulated by Craig Janney (15), Nelson Emerson (7), and Brendan Shanahan (19) in the 1993 playoffs. The Blues ousted Chicago from the playoffs in 1993 but were themselves eliminated in the second round.

be more accurate when using his forehand instead of his backhand. As Hull played the right wing, he was concerned that Oates would have more difficulty finding him because his center would not be passing to his natural side. But Oates wound up with 79 assists that season, so there turned out to be not much difficulty at all.

Hull, Oates, and the rest of the Blues finished the 1989-90 season with 83 points (a win is two points, a tie is one, and a loss is none). This was their highest total since they got 83 in 1985-86. But their playoffs ended in the second round with a loss to the Chicago Blackhawks in seven games. There was more work to do.

In the off-season, the Blues signed former Washington defenseman Scott Stevens to a free-agent contract. The move cost St. Louis five first-round draft picks, which meant that unless they made a trade, they would not be able to draft any college, Canadian junior, or European players in the first round for five straight years. Stevens was that good, so the Blues felt it was worth the risk.

When Hull signed his contract, Goodenow managed to get Blues management to throw in an incentive clause: if Hull won the Hart Trophy, the league's most valuable player award, Brett would get an extra $100,000. Management balked, but Goodenow and Hull wanted it in for only one season: the 1990-91 campaign. Management thought there was no way Hull would surpass Gretzky, Lemieux, and Detroit's Steve Yzerman in the voting, and they approved the clause.

Another loss for Blues management and another $100,000 for Hull.

The 1990-91 season was the high point of Brett Hull's career on a personal level. Nobody thought that he would repeat his efforts of the previous season and score another 72 goals. What Hull actually did was surpass that number to score the second-highest goal total in a season in NHL history, netting 86 goals! Only Gretzky has had more goals in a season—92 in 1991-92.

The 1990-91 season was when Hull got his 50 goals in 49 games. He wound up with 45 assists for a total of 131 points, while his linemate and buddy Oates finished 16 points behind him with 25 goals and 90 assists. Hull scored those 86 goals on 389 shots, giving him a shooting percentage of 22.1% (that's like scoring a goal once every five shots). Twenty-nine of those goals came on the power play. He had 11 game-winning goals and one game-tying goal.

Unfortunately, the ultimate goal for Hull and the Blues is winning the Stanley Cup, and again, the Blues exited the playoffs after losing their second-round series to the Minnesota North Stars.

Still, Hull did earn that Hart Trophy and the extra bonus money. "The award meant a great deal to me," Hull said. "My entire family was at the awards ceremonies in Toronto. Dad walked around the media room smoking a big cigar, like a proud father announcing the birth of a child."

Bobby was proud of his son, and his son knew it. "Everyone wants to follow in their father's footsteps, whether they are doctors, lawyers, or hockey players," Brett said. "Dad was one of the best, and I wanted to emulate him. Winning the award put me that much closer to doing that."

The comparisons end there, according to Brett. "Somebody asked me after I netted the 50-in-50 whether there would be any ribbing of Dad," Hull said. "Not a chance. Because all he has to say is, 'How many Stanley Cups have you won?'"

Ron Caron, the Blues' general manager, kept tinkering with his team, making bold moves that he thought would put the team over the edge and get them the Stanley Cup, but they just weren't enough to get the job done. Meanwhile, Hull scored 70, 54, and 57 goals in the next three seasons. In two of those three seasons, the Blues didn't make it past the first round of the playoffs, and in the one year they did (1993), they lost in the second round.

On February 7, 1992, Hull suffered a severe shock. Adam Oates, embroiled in a contract dispute with management, was traded to the Boston Bruins for Janney and defenseman Stephane Quintal. Hull, who had worked with Oates like a well-oiled machine, was losing not only his center but his best friend as well.

Hull slowly adapted to Janney, and Janney to Hull. In the following year, Janney actually led the team in scoring, with 24 goals and 82 assists for 106 points. Hull's 54 goals put him second on the team with 101 points, as he added 47 assists.

After losing to Dallas in the first round of the 1994 playoffs, Caron was almost out of ideas. Team owner Michael Shanahan had one, and it wouldn't suit Hull.

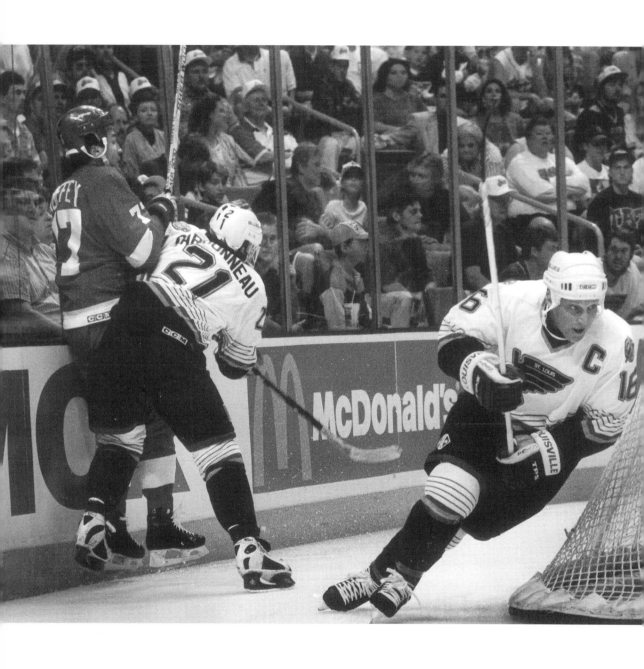

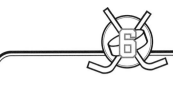

A DIFFERENT TUNE

The New York Rangers won the Stanley Cup in the 1993-94 season, the first time in 54 years they took the top prize. Their coach was Mike Keenan, who had a reputation for taking a team to a high level, but never being able to get them to the big prize. Keenan, who had previous coaching stints in Philadelphia and Chicago, coached by fear and motivation. He took teams in those cities and faced them in one direction: toward the Stanley Cup. Keenan's way would work for a few years in each city. Then the players would tune him out, and Keenan would have to find a fresh batch of troops to motivate.

Keenan was also a control addict. He wanted control of every little detail of a team and its operations. Ultimately, Keenan wanted to be the coach and general manager of a team. He never had the chance in Philadelphia, and in Chicago, he did hold both jobs, but not simultane-

Hull swoops around the net in a 1995 game against the Detroit Red Wings. Hull scored four goals in St. Louis's 6-5 victory.

51

St. Louis traded a lot of talent to the Los Angeles Kings to acquire Wayne Gretzky (right), but Hull (left) and the "Great One" were not teammates for long. Gretzky was not enamored with the Blues' front office and signed with the Rangers after his contract ran out.

ously. He wanted to get back into coaching so badly that he took the job with the Rangers, even though Neil Smith was already the general manager. Through a series of attempts, Keenan tried for Smith's job, but he failed to unseat him. So Keenan wanted out, and with a Stanley Cup championship freshly under his belt, he wanted to go somewhere where he could do both jobs. A contract snafu helped him escape his obligations in New York, and he immediately signed with the Blues.

Keenan was suspended for 60 days for his dealings with the Rangers, so he couldn't be at the start of training camp for the 1994-95 season, but he joined the team midway through the preseason. The team he inherited included stars such as Hull, Janney, Brendan Shanahan, Steve Duchesne, Phil Housley, and Curtis Joseph in goal.

Keenan was noted for wanting players to do things his way, or else they would be gone. With the exception of Hull, every player listed above was traded away within Keenan's first full season with the Blues. In fact, heading into the 1996-97 season, only Hull and defenseman Murray Baron remained from that 1993-94 team. During that period of time, Hull was given some top-notch centermen to work with, but Dale Hawerchuk was not Keenan's type of player, so he was dealt to Philadelphia.

In the 1992-93 season, Hull was elected to serve as team captain, which meant that he wore a letter "C" on the front of his uniform. It was quite an honor for Hull, who became the go-between when the coaches had a problem with a player or vice versa. He took his responsibility seriously, and it didn't affect his play in a negative way. The only thing it did affect was his already tenuous relationship with Keenan.

Hull was never much for being diplomatic when someone asked his opinion on anything, and as he saw a team that scored 91 points in 1993-94 being dismantled, he became upset. First, Janney, never a Keenan favorite for a perceived lack of intensity, was sent away to San Jose for defenseman Jeff Norton, which left Hull without a center to get him the puck. Then Keenan signed Hawerchuk as a free agent. Keenan also brought in some of his favorites from the Flyers, Blackhawks, and Rangers; those players were used to his style of coaching and had no problem with it. The names include Greg Gilbert, Glenn Anderson, Mike Hudson, and Brian Noonan. To his credit, Hull never missed a beat.

The NHL players were locked out by the owners, because the collective bargaining agreement between the players and the owners ran out and a new one had not been completed. After three months of tense negotiations between Goodenow and commissioner Gary Bettman, an agreement was reached in early January 1995. The league decided to go with a shortened schedule for that season, playing 48 games instead of the normal 82. Hull wound up scoring 29 goals under Keenan in those 48 games. Projected over a full 82-game season, Hull would have wound up with 50 goals. The Blues made the playoffs, but the results were no different under Keenan, as St. Louis bowed out in the first round, losing to the Vancouver Canucks in seven games.

Keenan got even busier during the off-season. First, he traded Shanahan, arguably the most popular player both on the team and with the fans, to Hartford for defenseman Chris Pronger. Eight days later, he traded Joseph and a prospect to the Edmonton Oilers for two draft picks. On the same day, he signed free agent Shayne Corson from those same Oilers, and traded Duchesne, an offensive-minded defenseman who played well on the power play, to the Ottawa Senators for another draft pick

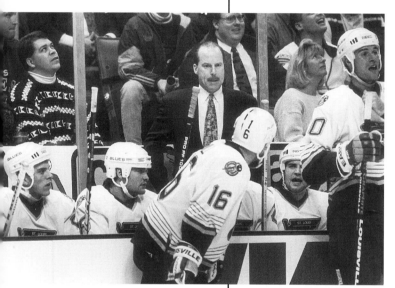

Coach Mike Keenan snarls instructions to Brett Hull in a 1995 game.

Within a year, Hull just about needed a scorecard to keep track of who was on his team. Keenan, who had little patience to begin with, never allowed his players the chance to work with each other and mesh. Hull complained. Keenan responded by stripping Hull of his captaincy and giving it to the newcomer Corson.

That move didn't do much for Hull's morale, but still, it didn't stop him from scoring 43 goals, the most of anyone on the team. Given the fact that the Blues scored only 219 goals overall, Hull accounted for just over 20 percent of the entire offensive output.

Despite having the team torn apart, Hull did have one period of happiness: on February 27, 1996, Wayne Gretzky, one of Hull's closest friends, became a St. Louis Blue. Keenan took a chance on getting "The Great Gretzky," trading away three youngsters (Roman Vopat, Patrice Tardif, and Craig Johnson) and two draft picks to Los Angeles to land him.

Nobody knows whether it was nerves, or a lack of playing together, but ironically, Hull had difficulties clicking with Gretzky like he did with Zezel, Oates, and Janney. Toward the end of the season and during the playoffs, the two meshed better. But the impatient Keenan would do something again to cause his team to self-destruct.

During the second round of the playoffs, Keenan ripped Gretzky after the team lost the second game of what would turn out to be a seven-game series against Detroit. Contract negotiations were also going on between Gretzky and the Blues to lock up Gretzky to a long-term deal. Inexplicably, Keenan pulled the offer off the table after that game. Those two instances proved insulting to arguably one of the greatest players in the game. After the season, Gretzky swore that he wouldn't sign with Keenan, no matter what money was being offered. True to his word, Gretzky signed a deal to play with the New York Rangers, rejoining old teammate Mark Messier. Both Gretzky and Messier were on the Edmonton Oilers team that won Stanley Cups in four of five seasons spanning 1984-1988.

As for Hull, he was angry at Keenan and vented his anger. "I wish I had season tickets for the Rangers," Hull said. "It would be fun to watch them play."

WORLD CUP AND THE FUTURE

Bobby Hull was born in Canada, as was Brett. Joanne Hull was born in the United States. Although Brett is a Canadian by birth, he is a citizen of both the U.S. and Canada.

When the 1996 World Cup tournament was formed, Hull could choose to play for either country. For Hull, the choice was easy. His decision came from an incident in 1986, when he turned pro and was set to play in the World Championship, an annual event that takes place at the end of the regular season.

"Both U.S. national team coach Dave Peterson and Canadian national team coach Dave King watched me play for UM-D," Hull said. "King didn't think I could skate well enough to play for Team Canada. Team USA general manager Art Berglund and Peterson invited me to play for them."

Ever since, Hull has always chosen the U.S. team. Every time he touched the puck in games

Hull hoists the World Cup of Hockey after the U.S. defeated Canada 5-2 on September 14, 1996.

Brett Hull's goal-scoring prowess sparked the United States at the 1996 World Cup.

played in Canada, however, the fans would chant "Traitor! Traitor!" To Hull, it was a question of loyalty, but to hockey fans throughout Canada, it was an answer of treason.

What was most painful to Canadian fans was that in September 1996, the U.S. and Canada met in the best two-out-of-three finals. In the preliminaries, the U.S. had won their match, but then came the first game of the finals, played in Philadelphia. Canada won a tight match in overtime. All they had to do was win one out of two possible games, both to be played on Canadian ice in Montreal. The U.S. won Game 2, forcing a deciding game. Canada broke a 1-1 tie with just over seven minutes left in the game, but Hull, who had scored the first goal, tied the game up, sparking a four-goal outburst to give the United States a 5-2 win and the Canada Cup trophy.

Indeed, Hull was the leading scorer for the tournament. He had seven goals (the most of any player on any of the eight teams in the tournament) and four assists, for 11 points in seven games. His last goal came as an empty netter— Canada had removed its goalie to put another offensive player on the ice. Ordinarily Hull disdains scoring a goal into an open cage, but he had no choice in this game. There was no one for him to pass the puck to, and his U.S. team needed an insurance goal.

After a natural high of winning the World Cup, he came back to another season with the Blues, his ninth with the team and third with Keenan.

Hull, never one to shy away from any topic, was in his usual form during the World Cup when asked about the state of the Blues. About Mike Keenan, he said, "How do you keep your job when you keep losing players? Someone has to be accountable for the state of the organization."

On losing Gretzky, he said, "It wasn't about money at all. There's only one reason Wayne's not in St. Louis and it's not too hard to figure out."

When asked if he thought he might be traded, he responded, "There's not a chance. I'm not going anywhere."

Team president Jack Quinn has promised that Hull will remain a fixture with the Blues. Hull loves the team, city, and fans. Chances of his staying improved when Mike Keenan was released during the 1996-97 season. Two days later, Hull celebrated by scoring his 500th goal, putting him in with the elite group of players that have reached that plateau. He and his father are the only family members to have achieved that status.

Hull has a summer home in the Duluth area, and continues to play for fun and money. His goal is to stop working after he retires from hockey—but there is one job he would take if offered: "Being athletic director at Minnesota-Duluth is about the only job that appeals to me as a post-NHL career," Hull said. "Otherwise, anyone who thinks I'm working a day after I retire from hockey is sadly mistaken."

STATISTICS

BRETT HULL

Regular Season

Season	Team	GP	G	A	PTS	PIM
1986-87	Calgary	5	1	0	1	0
1988-88	Calgary	52	26	24	50	12
	St. Louis	13	6	8	14	4
1988-89	St. Louis	78	41	43	84	33
1989-90	St. Louis	80	72	41	113	24
1990-91	St. Louis	78	86	45	131	22
1991-92	St. Louis	73	70	39	109	48
1992-93	St. Louis	80	54	47	101	41
1993-94	St. Louis	81	57	40	97	38
1994-95	St. Louis	48	29	21	50	10
1995-96	St. Louis	70	43	40	83	30
1996-97	St. Louis	77	42	40	82	10
TOTALS		735	527	388	915	272

Playoffs

Season	Team	GP	G	A	PTS	PIM
1985-86	Calgary	2	0	0	0	0
1986-87	Calgary	4	2	1	3	0
1987-88	St. Louis	10	7	2	9	4
1988-89	St. Louis	10	5	5	10	6
1989-90	St. Louis	12	13	8	21	17
1990-91	St. Louis	13	11	8	19	4
1991-92	St. Louis	6	4	4	8	4
1992-93	St. Louis	11	8	5	13	2
1993-94	St. Louis	4	2	1	3	0
1994-95	St. Louis	7	6	2	8	0
1995-96	St. Louis	13	6	5	11	10
1996-97	St. Louis	6	2	7	9	2
TOTALS		98	66	48	114	49

GP	games played
G	goals
A	assists
PTS	points
PIM	penalty minutes

BRETT HULL
A CHRONOLOGY

1964   Born on August 9 in Belleville, Ontario.

1983   Wins rookie of the year honors in the British Columbia Junior Hockey League with the Penticton Knights, breaking the record for most goals scored and most points in a season; drafted by the Calgary Flames.

1984   Enrolls at the University of Minnesota at Duluth.

1985   Leads the Bulldogs to a NCAA Final Four appearance.

1986   Signs a contract with the Calgary Flames; is first player ever to make his first pro appearance during the Stanley Cup finals.

1987   Plays most of the season with the Flames' minor league team in Moncton, New Brunswick; is named rookie of the year in the American Hockey League.

1988   Is traded to the St. Louis Blues.

1989   Scores 72 goals, a record for right wings.

1990   Signs a $7 million contract, third largest in the league.

1991   Scores 86 goals—second highest number ever; becomes sixth player ever to score 50 goals in 49 games; he and Bobby Hull become first ever father-son tandem each to score 50 goals in a season; wins Hart Trophy, for NHL's most valuable player.

1996   Leads U.S. to victory in the World Cup of Hockey; scores 500th career goal.

SUGGESTIONS FOR FURTHER READING

Goldstein, Margaret J. *Brett Hull: Hockey's Top Gun*. Minneapolis, MN: Lerner Publishing Co., 1992.

Hull, Brett, and Kevin Allen. *Brett*. Toronto, Ontario: McClelland & Stewart, 1991.

Ronberg, Gary. *The Ice Man*. New York: Crown Publishing, 1973.

ABOUT THE AUTHOR

Lou Friedman covers the New York Islanders, New York Rangers, and New Jersey Devils for a wide range of outlets including the *Associated Press*. He recently co-authored a book, *The New York Rangers: Broadway's Longest Running Hit*. He lives with his wife Denise on Long Island, NY.

PICTURE CREDITS: AP/Wide World Photos: 6, 12, 18, 38, 40, 43, 46, 50, 52, 54, 58; courtesy St. Louis Blues: 2; UPI/Corbis-Bettmann: 9, 14, 21; courtesy Sports Information Department, University of Minnesota, Duluth: 26, 29, 30, 33; Reuters/Mike Ridewood/Archive Press: 36.

INDEX